QUOTABLE
Casey

QUOTABLE Casey

The Wit, Wisdom, and Wacky Words of
CASEY STENGEL, Baseball's "Old Perfesser"
and Most Amazin' Manager

Fred McMane

TowleHouse Publishing
Nashville, Tennessee

TowleHouse books are distributed by National Book Network (NBN),
4720 Boston Way, Lanham, Maryland 20706.

Library of Congress Cataloging-in-Publication data is available.
ISBN: 0-931249-13-X

Cover design by Gore Studio, Inc.
Page design by Mike Towle

Printed in the United States of America
1 2 3 4 5 6 — 06 05 04 03 02

CONTENTS

INTRODUCTION

CHARLES DILLON "CASEY" STENGEL was, in baseball parlance, a late bloomer.

Although he broke into the major leagues as an outfielder in 1912, it wasn't until 1949, at the age of fifty-eight, that he really began to leave his mark on the sport. From 1949 through 1960, he managed the New York Yankees to ten American League pennants and seven World Series titles, including a record five in a row from 1949 to 1953.

Stengel had been a better-than-average player over fourteen major league seasons, yet as a manager he had few peers. He was astute, acerbic, and authoritative; he was also colorful, comical, and critical. He had keen insight into the game and a spongelike memory for everything, except people's names.

Ty Cobb, one of baseball's greatest players, called Stengel the greatest manager of all time. Connie Mack, himself a Hall of Fame manager, praised Stengel for his ability to juggle his lineup repeatedly while still getting the most out of his players.

Yet the general public more often saw the comical side of Casey. When he did not like a particular question and wanted to confuse an interviewer, he would make rambling, incoherent speeches, the content of which came to be known as "Stengelese."

Perhaps the moment that defined him most memorably in the eyes of the general public came on July 9, 1958, when Casey, then manager of the New York Yankees and already a forty-year veteran of professional baseball, was asked to appear before the U.S. Senate subcommittee on antitrust and monopoly in Washington, D.C.

Professional baseball still had its restrictive reserve clause, which bound a player to his contract for life. Some lawmakers believed that major league baseball was a monopoly and in violation of the historic Sherman Antitrust Act. At the time, baseball was pushing hard for the passage of a bill that would legally exempt the sport from antitrust restrictions in certain areas of its operation. Stengel, in Baltimore at the time for the All-Star Game, was asked to appear before the subcommittee along with several other baseball people, including Yankees star outfielder Mickey Mantle. Tennessee senator Estes Kefauver started the proceedings with a simple question.

"Mr. Stengel," said Senator Kefauver, "you are the manager of the New York Yankees. Will you give us very briefly your background and views about this legislation?"

Casey followed by delivering seven thousand words of pure Stengelese. His meanderings were occasionally interrupted by hearty laughter from the Senate floor and follow-up questions. When it was over, no one was quite sure what Stengel had said, but everyone knew that even the best of Senate fili-busters paled in comparison to Casey's verbosity. When he had finally finished, it was Mickey Mantle's turn to testify.

"Mr. Mantle," Kefauver asked, "do you have any obser-vations with reference to the applicability of the antitrust laws to baseball?"

"My views are just about the same as Casey's," Mantle replied.

"If you will redefine just what Casey's views were," the senator suggested, "we would be very happy."

Casey knew very well what he was saying . . . or not say-ing. On the subject of baseball, there were few minds as astute as his. However, he did not always want people to understand him.

"Stengelese was mostly a public act," said former New York Post baseball writer Maury Allen. "He double-talked in part to diffuse pinpoint questions. If you asked him who he was going to start at second base, he'd double-talk because he wouldn't want to decide until he made out his lineup ten minutes before the game. But he had a way of alerting the regular beat writers. If he veered off into talking about Rogers Hornsby, you knew he wanted an offensive second baseman for a high-scoring game. If he mentioned a good defensive player from years past, he wanted one for a low-scoring game."

When he wanted to, Casey would use perfect English that bore no resemblance to Stengelese. He could be a philosopher ("No one can explain winning or losing streaks."), a raconteur ("I was at a party one night and Casey was one of the guests," said former Yankees owner Del Webb. "He was in rare form. He had us standing around with our mouths open, putting on one of the best shows I've ever seen, telling stories, hopping around the room, mimicking other people."), and a self-deprecating comedian ("I feel greatly honored to have a ballpark named after me, especially since I been thrown out of so many ballparks.").

What Casey was most of all, though, was a keen observer of baseball talent with an uncanny knack for knowing how and when to use it. While he didn't invent platoon baseball, he was the first manager to use it extensively. He was famed for his against-the-book lineup changes, yet he was a master strategist and tactician.

Before he turned to managing, Casey played outfield for Brooklyn, Pittsburgh, the Philadelphia Phillies, the New York Giants, and the Boston Braves. He played fourteen seasons in the majors, compiling a respectable lifetime batting average of .284. He earned a measure of fame by hitting a game-winning, inside-the-park home run in Game One of the 1923 World Series, but he spent much of his career as a platoon player because of his inability to hit left-handed pitching well.

I

OPENING PITCHES

"I can make a living telling the truth."

A guy who has orange juice, cereal, bacon and eggs, toast and coffee, something like that, hasn't been fooling around all night. It's those guys who have double tomato juice and black coffee who've gone out to mail letters at three in the morning.[1]

⌒

A fly ball goes out there and you got two fellas in the outfield sayin', "I don't want it; you get it," and they bunk heads. I ain't seen no one die on a ball field chasin' balls.[2]

⌒

After the wedding I told the writers, "If you're going to print anything about us, you can say for the bridegroom that it is the best catch he ever made in his career."[3]

—*on his marriage to Edna*

⌒

All of you guys when you get into the locker room I want you to check your lockers. He stole everything out there he wanted today so he might have stolen your jocks as well.[4]

—after Brooklyn Dodgers star Jackie Robinson had run wild on the bases against the Yankees in an exhibition game in 1949

Without losers, where would winners be?[5]

All I ask is that you bust your heiny on that field.[6]

You got to get twenty-seven outs to win.[7]

Baseball is very big at the present time. This makes me think baseball will live longer than Casey Stengel or anybody else.[8]

Don't give up. Tomorrow is another day, and that's myself.[9]

Even two writers have deposits—$15 or $20. Their life savings.[10]

—*about his bank in Glendale*

I don't really need this, but I have to limp or I can't get into the Hall of Fame.[11]

—*after hip surgery required him to walk with a cane in 1965*

Yeah? For what paper?[12]

—on being told that Ernest Hemingway was a great writer

I feel greatly honored to have a ballpark named after me, especially since I've been thrown out of so many.[13]

I don't like them fellas who drive in two runs and let in three.[14]

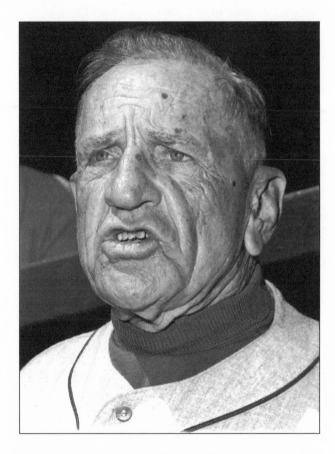

Let the Stengelese roll! (AP/Wide World Photos)

I love signing autographs. I'll sign anything but veal cutlets. My ballpoint pen slips on veal cutlets.[15]

~

I am pleased to accept this award from you gentlemen and am fortunate to be able to make a career in baseball, which is important, because as you know, not many people would actually have put their trust in a left-handed dentist.[16]

~

I'm a man that's been up and down.[17]

~

It ain't getting it that hurts them, it's staying up all night looking for it. They gotta learn that if you don't get it by midnight, you ain't gonna get it, and if you do it ain't worth it.[18]

—on chasing women

People ask me, "Casey, how can you speak so much when you don't talk English too good?" Well, I've been invited to Europe, and I say, "They don't speak English over there too good, either."[19]

A shave, please, but don't cut my throat. I may want to do it later myself.[20]

—to his barber, while managing the Brooklyn Dodgers in 1935

Left-handers have more enthusiasm for life. They sleep on the wrong side of the bed and their head gets more stagnant on that side.[21]

Mister, that boy couldn't hit the ground if he fell out of an airplane.[22]

No, even my players aren't players.[23]

Old-timers' weekends and airplane landings are alike. If you can walk away from them, they're successful.[24]

Sometimes I get a little hard-of-speaking.[25]

Sure holds the heat well.[26]

        —on the new Busch Stadium in St. Louis in 1966 where
the All-Star game was played in 113-degree heat on the artificial turf

The trouble with women umpires is that I couldn't argue with one. I'd put my arms around her and give her a little kiss.[27]

The only woman which has been in my life. She has been splendid.[28]

        —about his wife Edna

The way our luck has been lately, our fellas have been getting hurt on their days off.[29]

This is a five-story building in Glendale. Here at first base is the branch at Burbank. At second base, North Hollywood. You come around third—no bank there—and you're back home. You run the bases on the freeway and there I am sitting in front of the vault guarding the money.[30]

—about his banking career following his career in baseball

Throw ground balls . . . throw those sinkers. Make 'em hit ground balls. Never heard anyone gettin' home runs on ground balls.[31]

We got clean uniforms if you get 'em dirty. Why, the owners is just dyin' to have you get 'em dirty; I like to see 'em dirty. There's laundries. You tear a uniform, they just waitin' to take it right off and give you another one.[32]

When I don't win, I'm good and mad at night. But if you think you're going to do better just by being serious all the time and never telling any stories or doing any kidding around—why, you're a little mistaken. Some people could never understand that.[33]

When you're losing, everyone commences to playing stupid.[34]

When I played in Brooklyn, I could go to the ballpark for a nickel carfare. But now I live in Pasadena, and it costs me fifteen or sixteen dollars to take a cab to Glendale. If I was a young man, I'd study to become a cabdriver.[35]

—*after his retirement in 1965*

He went out to mail a letter.[36]

> —*explaining why pitcher Don Larsen was out at
> 5:00 A.M. when he wrecked his car, during spring training*

⁓

I'm in jail. Y'gotta come down and bail me out. It's
fifty dollars, but bring more because they might
change their mind.[37]

> —*calling on a jail phone to the team's PR man
> after being arrested for allegedly kicking a photographer*

⁓

I have great respect for veterans, having been one
myself from the navy in World World I, and you can
look it up.[38]

⁓

Are they going to frisk us first?[39]

> —*to wife Edna when he once attended Catholic Mass
> with her and saw the collection plate coming a second time*

⁓

I don't play cards,
I don't play golf,
and I don't go to
the picture show.
All that's left is
baseball.[40]

2

THE OLD
PERFESSER

"Call me and I'll give y'all the answers."

As great as the other men were on the ball club, there comes a time when you get a weakness and it might be physical.[1]

⌒

All right, everybody line up alphabetically according to your height.[2]

⌒

Call me and I'll give y'all the answers.[3]

⌒

Don't drink in the hotel bar. That's where I do my drinking.

⌒

Good pitching will always stop good hitting and vice versa.

⌒

I want to thank all the players for giving me the opportunity of being what I was.[4]

⌒

I can make a living telling the truth.[5]

⌒

I was a left-handed dentist who made people cry. I was not very good at pulling teeth, but my mother loved my work. Some of the people in the clinic didn't share her views.[6]

I was improving my sliding out there, but one day the manager told me something that made me stop. What he told me was this: "See that brick house on the hill beyond the fence? Well, that's a nut house, and if the fellow that runs it ever sees you, he'll come in here and throw a net over you, and I'm not sure it wouldn't be a good idea at that."[7]

Now there's three things you can do in a baseball game. You can win, you can lose, or it can rain.[8]

I see a lot of you guys reading about the stock market, and I know you're thinking about it. Now, I'm gonna do you a favor, since you're so interested in Wall Street. I'm gonna give you a tip on the market. Buy Pennsylvania Railroad—because if you don't start playing better ball there's gonna be so many of you riding trains outta here that railroad stocks are a cinch to go up.[9]

—as manager of the Toledo Mud Hens

If you're so smart, let's see you get out of the army.[10]

—a telegram sent by Stengel to a
soldier who had criticized Stengel's managing

It's high time something was done for the pitchers. They put up the stands and take down fences to make more home runs and plague the pitchers. Let them revive the spitter and help the pitchers make a living.[11]

It's wonderful to meet so many friends that I didn't used to like.[12]

Just because your legs is dead don't mean your head is.[13]

Midgets are smart. Smart and slick as eels. You know why? It's because they're not able to do much with those short fingers. You understand? Not being able to do anything with their fingers, what do they do? They develop their brain power.[14]

Some men are quiet but ambitious. Some are quiet and don't talk. They won't tell you what their troubles are in playing ball. If you can get a man to talk to you, then you can find out real quick what's wrong with him.[15]

There comes a time in every man's life at least once, and I've had plenty of them.[16]

There's not much of a secret to platooning. You put a right-hand hitter against a left-hand pitcher and a left-hand hitter against a right-hand pitcher and on cloudy days you use a fastball pitcher.[17]

We are in such a slump that even the ones that are drinkin' aren't hittin'.

The Old Perfesser contemplates the seventh game of the 1960 World Series against the Pittsburgh Pirates. It would turn out to be Stengel's last game as Yankees manager. (AP/Wide World Photos)

You make your own luck. Some people have bad luck all their lives.[18]

⌒

Well, that's baseball. Rags to riches one day and riches to rags the next. But I've been in it thirty-six years and I'm used to it.[19]

⌒

Well, to be perfectly truthful and honest and frank about it, the thing I'd like to be right now is . . . an astronaut.[20]

—when asked if he'd like to go back to managing

⌒

You have to go broke three times to learn how to make a living.[21]

⌒

3

HIS AGE AND HEALTH

"Most people my age are dead at the present time."

I don't like to talk about a person's age, see? I'd rather talk about his experiences and qualifications, such as either you've got 'em or you don't, and then let age take care of itself. Except in this society, it don't always work this way.[1]

I'd rather

Why should I be old-fashioned just because I'm old?[2]

Most people my age are dead at the present time.[3]

—*on turning seventy in 1960*

My health is good enough about the shoulders.[4]

A wheelchair wasn't available, so a cane had to do.
(AP/Wide World Photos)

Nuts to being old. I'll try to manage as long as I don't have to go to take a pitcher out in a wheelchair.[5]

~

That's where they opened me up to put that plastic ball in the socket of the hip. I don't know if it's a National League ball or an American League ball.[6]

—*after undergoing hip-replacement surgery in August of 1965*

I stayed up last night and watched the Republican Convention all night long. I watched all of them talk and listened to them and seen them, and I'm not interested in politics. If you watch them and listen to them, you find out why.[7]

The trick is growing up without growing old.[8]

~

They examined all my organs. Some of them are quite remarkable and others are not so good. A lot of museums are bidding for them.[9]

—after being hospitalized for two weeks during spring training in 1960

~

Once someone gave me a picture, and I wrote, "Do good in school." I looked up and the guy was seventy-eight years old.[10]

~

4

HIS PLAYING DAYS

"I chased the balls that Babe Ruth hit."

The real Casey at the bat. (Courtesy of New York Yankees)

I broke in with four hits and the writers promptly declared they had seen the new Ty Cobb. It took me only a few days to correct that impression.

I was such a dangerous hitter, I even got intentional walks in batting practice.[1]

I made six hits and a couple of tremendous catches in the outfield. I am so fast I overrun one base and am tagged out. I steal a couple of bases, which is embarrassing for me because there's already runners on them.[2]

I was fairly good at times, but a lot of people seem to remember some of the stunts I pulled better than they do the ball games I helped win.[3]

I chased the balls that Babe Ruth hit.[4]

⌒

It used to be that you had to catch the ball two-handed because the glove was so small. Why, when I got married I couldn't afford dress gloves, so I wore my baseball mitt to my wedding and nobody noticed. That took care of my right hand, and I was smart enough to keep my left hand in my pocket.[5]

⌒

It was rougher then. . . . When I broke in, you just knew they were throwing at you. The first month I was in the league, I spent three weeks on my back at the plate.[6]

⌒

My platoon thinking started with the way (John) McGraw handled me in my last years on the Giants. He had me in and out of the lineup, and he used me all around the outfield. He put me in when and where he thought I could do the most good. And, after I got into managing, I platooned whenever I had the chance, long before I came to the Yankees.[7]

The Youth of America. You say, "Here is the opportunity," and the Youth of America says, "How much are you going to pay me?"[8]

The higher-ups complained I wasn't showing a serious attitude by hiding a sparrow in my hat, but I said any day I get three hits, I figure I am showing a more serious attitude than a lot of players with no sparrows in their hat.[9]

They brought me up to the Brooklyn Dodgers, which at that time was in Brooklyn.[10]

I mighta been able to make it as a pitcher except for one thing: I had a rather awkward motion, and every time I brought my left arm forward I hit myself in the ear.[11]

Wake up muscles, we're in New York now.[12]

—*upon being traded to the Giants from the Phillies in 1921*

With the salary I get here, I'm so hollow and starvin' that I'm liable to explode like a light bulb if I hit the ground too hard.[13]

—*when he was with Pittsburgh in 1918*

Whaddya mean, nuts? I'm practicin', I'm throwin', runnin', and slidin', ain't I?[14]

—referring to his habit when taking the field of throwing his glove toward center field, sprinting toward it, and then sliding into it

If you want somebody to play the angles, why don't you hire a pool player?[15]

—response to his minor league manager in 1910 criticizing his outfield play around the fences

Your ears are too big. I can't see the ball leave the bat.[16]

—telling a teammate pitcher about the difficulty in trying to play center field when he's pitching

I made like a bee or fly was bothering me, so I kept rubbing the end of my nose, with my fingers pointing toward the Yankees dugout. I heard about that in a hurry. Commissioner (Kenesaw Mountain) Landis called me over and said he didn't like that kind of exhibition before sixty thousand people, and he told me, "If you do that again, I promise you one thing: You won't receive a dollar of your World Series shares."[17]

—explaining why he was supposedly thumbing his nose at the opposing Yankees after hitting a home run for the Giants in the 1923 World Series

My name is Stengel. Take a good look at me because I'm going to be around a long time.[18]

5

MANAGING

"You don't copy another manager unless you want to get fired."

Brooklyn was the borough of churches and bad ball clubs, many of which I had.[1]

～

Handling kids involves not only how to teach, but what to teach them. This calls for drawing up a comprehensive schedule and detailing certain jobs to certain men. That's why our preliminary camps are so successful. Competent specialists instruct in definite fields.[2]

～

How can any manager make mistakes when he hasn't had a base runner for eighteen innings?[3]

～

I got players with bad watches—they can't tell midnight from noon.[4]

～

Taking it all in as manager of the minor-league Boston Bees, in 1941. (AP/Wide World Photos)

I came in here and a fella asked me to have a drink. I said I don't drink. Then another fella said, "Hear you and Joe DiMaggio aren't speaking," and I said, "I'll take that drink."[5]

$\backsim$

I couldn't have done it without my players.[6]
—*on winning the 1958 World Series*

$\backsim$

I'm the fella in charge. It's kinda like being the mother superior.[7]
—*explaining his job to a nun*

$\backsim$

If you're playing baseball and thinking about managing, you're crazy. You'd be better off thinking about being an owner.[8]

$\backsim$

If this keeps up (four-game winning streak), I'm about to manage until I'm a hundred.[9]

If we're going to win the pennant, we've got to start thinking we're not as good as we think we are.[10]

Managing is getting paid for home runs someone else hits.[11]

Most ball games are lost, not won.

Nobody ever had too many of them (pitchers).[12]

Percentage isn't just strategy. It's execution. If a situation calls for a bunt and you have a batter who can't bunt, what's the percentage of bunting?[13]

Playing your infield in turns a .200 hitter into a .300 hitter.[14]

⌐

The secret of managing a club is to keep the five guys who hate you from the five who are undecided.[15]

⌐

The Yankees don't pay me to win every day, just two out of three.[16]

⌐

We're playing twenty-five men, we might as well let them earn their money.[17]

⌒

You can't go out to the mound hobbling and take a pitcher out with a cane.[18]

⌒

You don't copy another manager unless you want to get fired.[19]

⌒

You know, John McGraw was a great man in New York and he won a lot of pennants. But Stengel is in town now, and he's won a lot of pennants, too.[20]

—*after winning his fifth straight World Series in 1953*

What do I say when I go out to take the
pitcher out? I usually say, "Hello, darling.
How are you this evening?"[21]

⌒

Whenever I decided to release a guy, I always
had his room searched first for a gun. You
couldn't take any chances with some of them
birds.[22]

⌒

Keep your eyes off the scoreboard. Keep them
on your own game. Pay attention to your own
game.[23]

⌒

Every so often you have to get to certain individuals. When they're going bad, it's no time to jump on someone's back, because you might get punched in the nose. But when they're winning and they're not going well, they'll listen to you, and they'll absorb more.[24]

6

PLAYERS

*"He's the perdotious quotient
of the qualificatilus."*

(Paul) Waner had to be a very graceful player, because he could slide without breaking the bottle on his hip.[1]

—about Waner's alleged fondness for alcohol

~

(Rogers) Hornsby could run like anything but not like this kid (Mickey Mantle). Cobb was the fastest I ever saw for being sensational on the bases.[2]

~

Fine him? He oughta get an award, finding something to do in this town after midnight.[3]

—after learning pitcher Don Larsen had crashed his car into a telephone pole at 5:00 A.M.

~

Nobody knows this [yet], but one of us has just been traded to Kansas City.[4]

—to outfielder Bob Cerv

He (Satchel Paige) threw the ball as far from the bat and as close to the plate as possible.[5]

He was as good a curveball hitter as anybody ever saw, then or now. In fact, he was so good that John J. McGraw had a rule, which was that any Giants pitcher who threw Mr. Wheat a curveball would get fined $500, or be shipped to Peoria, which was almost as bad.[6]

—on Hall of Famer Zach Wheat

He (Babe Ruth) was very brave at the plate. You rarely saw him fall away from a pitch. He stayed right in there. No one drove him out.[7]

He's an unusual hitter. Sometimes he stands straight up, and sometimes his head is so close to the plate he looks like John the Baptist.[8]

He's the perdotious quotient of the qualificatilus. He's the lower intestine.[9]

—*on Don Zimmer*

I don't know when they're going to learn.[10]

He's throwing
grounders.

I never saw anyone like (Ty) Cobb. No one even close to him. When he wiggled those wild eyes at a pitcher, you knew you were looking at the one bird nobody could beat.[11]

⌒

I had this player in Brooklyn, and you could ask him for a match and find out what bar he was in the night before. After we traded him to another club, I always went up to him before the game and asked for a match. If he pulled out a match from some bar, I knew he had been out late and I could pitch him fastballs.[12]

⌒

I don't want to get involved with (Jackie) Robinson. He was a great ballplayer once. But everyone knows that he's now Chock Full o' Nuts.[13]

—about charges made by Robinson, who went to work for a coffee company after retiring from baseball, that Stengel was a racist

I'd love to leave you in, but I got too many married men in the infield.[14]

—speaking to reporters in 1950 in spring training about a game the previous season when Allie Reynolds was knocked around by the Red Sox

If Ted Williams could see the ball so good up at the plate, then why don't umpires stand sideways to call balls and strikes?[15]

Johnny Sain don't say much, but that don't matter much, because when you're out there on the mound, you got nobody to talk to.

⌒

Look at him. He don't smoke, he don't drink, he don't chase women, and he don't win.[16]

—*on pitcher Bob Turley*

⌒

Some of my players think he's a show-off. That's because every time they see him he's running.[17]

—*on Enos Slaughter*

⌒

Some people say this man is crazy. Well, he certainly doesn't play crazy. When he hits the ball he never runs to third base. He doesn't run through the pitcher's box either.[18]

—on Boston Red Sox outfielder Jimmy Piersall, who suffered a nervous breakdown early in his career

Son, we'd like to keep you around this season, but we're going to try and win a pennant.[19]

—breaking the news to a player that he is being cut

Stop that, if you break a toe I won't be able to get anything for you.[20]

—on Brooklyn pitcher "Boom Boom" Beck

That fella runs splendid but he needs help at the plate which coming from country chasing rabbits all winter give him strong legs although he broke one falling out of a tree which shows you can't tell and when a curveball comes he waves at it and if pitchers don't throw curves you have no pitching staff so how is a manager going to know whether to tell boys to fall out of trees and break legs so he can run fast even if he can't hit a curveball.[21]

—*classic rambling Stengelese*

Looks like some serious managing going on here.
(Courtesy of New York Yankees)

They got a lot of kids now whose uniforms are so tight, especially the pants, that they cannot bend over to pick up ground balls. And they don't want to bend over in television games because in that way there is no way their face can get on the camera.[22]

They say some of my stars drink whiskey, but I have found that ones who drink milk shakes don't win many ball games.[23]

When you got four first basemen, you got no first baseman.[24]

—*speaking to* New York Times *writer Leonard Koppett in 1949*

Ya don't listen to what the players say because the ones which is mad at you can win the most games.[25]

Yer too small. Ga wan. Go home. Get a shoebox.[26]

—to five-foot-five shortstop Phil Rizzuto, a future Hall of Famer, after a tryout for the Brooklyn Dodgers in 1935

You put the whammy on him, but when he's (Sandy Koufax) pitching, the whammy tends to go on vacation.[27]

He (Babe Ruth) would hit a pop-up so high, that everyone on the field thought he had a chance to get it. They'd all try to get under to make the catch, and it looked like a union meetin'.[28]

7

THE YANKEES

"The name Yankees stands for
something all over the world."

Brown reminds me of a fellow who's been hitting for twelve years and fielding one.[1]

> —*on third baseman Bobby Brown, in 1951*

Doggone it, that kid (Mickey Mantle) will never understand. I know how to do it because I used to play baseball myself. What he thinks is that I was born sixty years old.[2]

Every time he wins a game, people come down out of the stands asking for contracts.[3]

> —*on junkballing pitcher Eddie Lopat*

He takes a drink or ten, comes in with those coke bottles (thick glasses), throws one on the screen, and scares the (stuff) out of 'em.[4]

—on relief pitcher Ryne Duren

He (Mickey Mantle) has it in his body to be great.[5]

He watches all the sports and knows about them all. If he turned on the television, Yogi would watch it and pretty soon he would know what makes the skates roll.[6]

He talks okay up there with a bat in his hands. A college education don't do you no good up there.[7]

—*on Yogi Berra*

He (Mickey Mantle) should lead the league in everything. With his combination of speed and power he should win the triple batting crown every year. In fact, he should do anything he wants to do.[8]

He (Jerry Lumpe) looks like the greatest hitter in the world until you play him.[9]

He'd fall in a sewer
and come up with
a gold watch.[10]

—on catcher Yogi Berra

I commenced winning pennants as soon as I got here, but I did not commence getting any younger.[11]

⌒

I would not admire hitting against Ryne Duren, because if he ever hit you in the head you might be in the past tense.

⌒

I come from the West Coast, and they all say the weather is pretty good out there, but I like it fine here, and if some of my players act as if they don't want to be here, I will change my ideas and trade some and see how well they like it out of this big city where they lived a little better than they ever lived before.[12]

⌒

I think everybody on the club should fly except the scouts. We can't afford to fly our scouts—too many small airfields where they go. We don't want to lose any scouts, for there's a rebuilding program. I think it would be better if we made them just use buses.[13]

I'll never make the mistake of being seventy again.[14]
—after he was fired by the Yankees following the 1960 season

I'm with a lot of real pros. When I think of some of those other teams I had, I was wondering whether I was managing a baseball team or a golf course. You know what I mean—one pro to a club.[15]
—on taking over as manager of the Yankees in 1949

If I don't win the pennant this year, they oughta commence firing the manager.[16]

—in the spring of 1954

⌒

Look at him, he's always watching the ball. He isn't watching second base. He isn't watching third base. He knows they haven't been moved. He isn't watching the ground because he knows they haven't built a canal or a swimming pool since he was last there. He's watching the ball and the outfielder, which is the one thing that is different on every play.[17]

—on Joe DiMaggio

⌒

Make 'em pay you a thousand dollars. Don't go help those people with their shows for coffee-and-cake money. You're the Yankees—the best. Make 'em pay you high.[18]

—to his players on the subject of personal appearances

⌒

Right now we're playin' bad every place. Not hittin', not pitchin', and not fieldin' too good. And judgin' by what I read in the newspapers, the Yankee writers are in a slump, too.[19]

Stengel and "the Mick." (Courtesy of New York Yankees)

The name *Yankees* stands for something all over the world. You players play every game over here as if your job depended on it. It just might.[20]

—*with the Yankees in Japan*

There ain't nothing he don't think he can do. He thinks he knows more about baseball than anybody else, and it wouldn't surprise me if he was right.[21]

—*on Billy Martin*

There's been a lot of fast men but none as big and strong as (Mickey) Mantle. He's gonna be around a long time, if he can stay well, that fella of mine.[22]

There's never been anything like this kid which we got from Joplin. He has more speed than any slugger and more slug than any speedster—and nobody has ever had more of both of 'em together.[23]

—*on Mickey Mantle, in 1950*

They say he's (Yogi Berra) funny. Well, he has a lovely wife and family, a beautiful home, money in the bank, and he plays golf with millionaires. What's funny about that?[24]

Well, do you remember DiMaggio ever diving for a ball? He had an uncanny start. It looked like he could go after a ball at the sound of an echo.[25]

Well, I made up my mind, but I made it up both ways.[26]

*—when asked in 1960 if he would quit as
manager if the Yankees lost the World Series to the Pirates*

Well, it's like this. When we lose in the afternoon, I don't feel good that night. When we lose at night, I don't feel good in the morning, even after I've had breakfast. Maybe I just don't like to lose.[27]

What do I care what the AP (Associated Press) says? Their opinion ain't gonna send me into a faint. What did the UP (United Press) say?[28]

—on wire service report that he had been fired by the Yankees

What the Yankees have that's great is the guy (Pete Sheehy) that takes care of the clubhouse. He keeps it so neat I'm afraid to let Edna see it. She'll make me work around the house.[29]

Why has our pitching been so great? Our catcher (Yogi Berra), that's why. He looks cumbersome, but he's quick as a cat.[30]

⌒

Yogi looks like he can't run, but when they bunt the ball in front of the plate, he jumps at it like he just spotted a silver dollar on the ground.[31]

⌒

That kid (Mantle) hits them pretty far. The stratmosphere around here helps.[32]

—referring to Arizona's hot, dry air that supposedly helped the ball carry farther

⌒

It's true I used to fall asleep on the Yankees bench. We were so efficient, it put me to sleep.[33]

⌒

I'd like to put you in there, but if I do, I won't have you on the bench to pinch-hit. So I think I'll keep you on the bench until I need you.[34]

—to veteran slugger Johnny Mize, whose best hitting days were behind him by the time he got to the Yankees

⌒

Joe DiMaggio was the greatest player I ever had. . . . He was the best player because he could execute all the plays. He could play center field, get a start on the ball; he could field, throw. On base he used good sound judgment.[35]

⌒

We fought over some things, but he never stopped paying me. If your checks don't bounce, why wouldn't you like the man?[36]

—referring to Yankees general manager George Weiss

⌒

Yogi Berra's one of my only players that's never been booed but once in his life. He's an odd character. He looked like a wrestler.[37]

Every year I get these young shortstops and they always tell me they're ready for the Yankees. . . . They all say they can do it like Rizzuto did, but did you know something? There ain't a one of them can.[38]

That little punk—how I love 'im![39]

—*talking about Billy Martin*

~

He has more speed than any slugger, and more slug than any speedster.[40]

—*talking about Mickey Mantle*

~

The best thing he (DiMaggio) had—and I'll give you a tip—was his head.[41]

~

8

THE AMAZIN' METS

"If anybody wants me,
tell them I'm being embalmed."

Amazing strength, amazing power—he (Ron Swoboda) can grind the dust out of the bat. He will be great, super, wonderful. Now, if he can only learn to catch a fly ball.[1]

And in left field, in left field, we have a splendid man, and he knows how to do it. He's been around and he swings the bat there in left field and he knows what to do. He's got a big family (six children) and he wants to provide for them, and he's a fine outstanding player, the fella in left field. You can be sure he'll be ready when the bell rings—and that's his name, Bell![2]

> —*trying to remember outfielder*
> *Gus Bell's name prior to opening day in 1962*

He wanted to see poverty, so he came to see my team.[3]

—referring to President Lyndon Johnson's 1964 visit to see the Mets

⁓

He (Gil Hodges) fields better on one leg than anybody else I got on two.[4]

—on why he elected to start the aging first baseman over some younger players in 1962

You have to have a catcher, because if you don't, you're likely to have a lot of passed balls.[5]

—on the Mets' taking catcher Hobie Landrith with their first pick in the 1962 expansion draft

He's a remarkable catcher, that Canzoneri. He's the only defensive catcher in baseball that can't catch.[6]

—evaluating reserve catcher Chris Cannizzaro

Hey (Don) Heffner, take them down to that other field (Saint Petersburg spring training site). I want to see if they can play on the road.[7]

~

I been in this game a hundred years, but I see new ways to lose I never knew existed before.[8]

~

I got a lot of keys to a lot of cities, but this one I'm gonna use to open a new team.[9]

—after receiving a key to New York City during a welcoming parade up Broadway before the 1962 season

~

I got one that can throw but can't catch, and one that can catch but can't throw, and one who can hit but can't do either.[10]

~

I got the smartest pitcher in the world until he goes to the mound.[11]

> —on Mets pitcher Jay Hook,
> a Northwestern University graduate

I got this broken arm from watching my team. All they gave me last year was a head cold.[12]

> —after falling down a concrete ramp and
> breaking his arm during the 1965 season

I'm sorta glad (the 1962 Mets) didn't yell at the umpires. We'd probably have won only fifteen.[13]

> —after his first-year expansion team finished with a 40-120 record

Strangers are hard to manage. It was like spring training all year. But I expected to win more games. I was very much shocked.[14]

If anybody wants me, tell them I'm being embalmed.[15]

*—after an all-night flight from Milwaukee to Houston
in 1962 that didn't get the Mets to their hotel room until 8:00 A.M.*

It couldn't have been a perfect pitch. Perfect pitches don't travel that far.[16]

*—to Mets pitcher Ray Daviault after Daviault insisted he threw a
perfect pitch that Cardinals outfielder Charley James hit for a
long, game-winning home run during an early-season 1962 game*

It's a great honor for me to be joining the Knickerbockers.[17]

—on being named the first Mets manager, October 2, 1961

Look at that guy. He can't hit, he can't run, and he can't throw. Of course, that's why they gave him to us.[18]

The floral horseshoe wasn't lucky for Casey on April 13, 1962: The Mets lost to the Pirates, 4-3, at the Polo Grounds. (AP/Wide World Photos)

Lovely, just lovely. The park is lovelier than my team.[19]

—*on the opening of Shea Stadium in 1963*

⌒

My hitters have complained about the bad background here for three years and they've only played here one day.[20]

—*about the Mets' reaction to the new Shea Stadium in 1964*

⌒

My face alone will pack the Polo Grounds the first year.[21]

⌒

Now just make believe you're pitching against Harvard.[22]

> —*after calling Yale graduate Ken MacKenzie into a tight game for the Mets*

Now I'll tell you what to do. You go and buy those baseballs and then you'll give them to me and I'll take them to the clubhouse and get my amazing Mets to sign their names on them and that'll be good practice for them writing checks when they start to make all that money that my owners have.[23]

The only thing worse than a Mets game is a Mets doubleheader.[24]

There is a fellow who could find me a nice vacancy
to live (in) if this club finishes last.[25]

—*referring to astronaut John Glenn*

They really gave it to us. They sold us all the disabled
players they had.[26]

—*on the building of the Mets*

This club (the '69 Mets) plays better baseball now.
Some of them look fairly alert.[27]

This here team won't go anywhere unless we spread
enough of our players around the league and make
the other teams (terrible), too.[28]

—*after the Mets finished the 1964 season with a 53-109 record*

We didn't get him in the draft, but you could say he was the most valuable man we had last year. If it hadn't been for him, some of our players who are helping us this year wouldn't even be around now. You know, sometimes I wish he could hit.[29]

—*on the Mets' team physician Dr. Peter LaMotte*

We are a much-improved ball club; now we lose in extra innings![30]

We were damn lucky (the National League) didn't expand to twelve teams.[31]

—*after his expansion Mets lost 120 games in 1962*

We ain't doing so good, but we're sure trying.[32]

We got the young people, twelve to fourteen years old, and some were eighteen, and their parents would have to come to hold some of the banners. And if a banner got in your way, you didn't mind missing a play because it was something bad happening and why would you want to see it?[33]

The attendance was robbed. We're still a fraud.[34]

> —*after the Mets were shut out, 7-0, by the*
> *St. Louis Cardinals on Opening Day 1963*

⌒

We've (the '62 Mets) got to learn to stay out of triple plays.[35]

⌒

You're full of baloney; he can run the bases.[36]

> —*responding to general manager George Weiss's comment*
> *that prospect Rod Kanehl couldn't "do anything in the field"*

⌒

Most of our hitters are what? Putsie-downsies.[37]

> —*referring to his Mets' weak-hitting swings*

⌒

Well, we've got this Johnny Lewis in the outfield. They hit a ball to him yesterday, and he turned left, then he turned right, then he went straight back and caught the ball. He made three good plays in one. And Greg Goossen, he's only twenty years old and with a good chance in ten years of being thirty.[38]

What am I supposed to do about the plumbers I got down there?[39]

—*talking about the Mets bullpen in 1964*

You couldn't play on my Amazin' Mets without having held some kind of record, like one fella held the world's international all-time record for a pitcher getting hit on the ankles.[40]

Yeah, and he's got the highest earned-run average, too.[41]

> —*when informed that pitcher Ken MacKenzie was the lowest-paid member of the Yale class of 1956*

～

You would think he was a player if he wasn't left-handed.[42]

> —*about Mets pitcher Al Jackson*

～

When we first started, we had to take players nobody else wanted anymore or at all. One time I looked over at the Dodgers who had Mr. Koufax and Mr. Drysdale pitching and Mr. Wills running and I said, "They're mahogany over there and we're driftwood."[43]

～

Ninety-nine more like that and we win the pennant.[44]

—after his 1962 Mets team won their first
game on April 23 after opening with nine straight losses

9

OTHERS ON CASEY

*"I played for Casey before
and after he was a genius."*

—WARREN SPAHN

CASEY HAS FORGOTTEN MORE BASEBALL THAN I EVER
KNEW. THAT'S THE TROUBLE, HE'S FORGOTTEN IT.[1]
—*Jimmy Piersall*

CASEY COULD FOOL YOU. WHEN HE WANTED TO MAKE
SENSE HE COULD. BUT HE USUALLY PREFERRED TO MAKE
YOU LAUGH. THAT'S WHY HE SPOKE STENGELESE.[2]
—*Yogi Berra*

CASEY WAS THE BEST PUBLIC-RELATIONS MAN WHO EVER
LIVED. HE KNEW EXACTLY WHAT HE WAS DOING ALL
THE TIME.[3]
—*Whitey Herzog*

CASEY MAY NOT WIN THE PENNANT, BUT YOU CAN BET
HE'LL LEAVE US LAUGHING WHEN HE SAYS GOOD-BYE.[4]
—*unidentified sportswriter, 1949*

HE WOULD TALK ABOUT GAME SITUATIONS FROM FORTY YEARS AGO, AND I WAS TWENTY AT THE TIME. ON A COUPLE OF OCCASIONS HE CAUGHT MY EYE WHEN HE WAS GOING INTO THOSE VERBAL MEANDERS. HE WOULD TALK IN PARABLES. NEXT THING YOU KNOW HE WAS TALKING ABOUT A PLAYER WHO WAS INVOLVED IN A SITUATION THAT APPLIED TO A SITUATION HE HAD BEEN TALKING TO YOU ABOUT. YOU REALIZED THE STORY WAS FOR YOU.[5]

—*Ron Swoboda*

HE DOESN'T TALK ABOUT ANYTHING ELSE, HE DOESN'T THINK ABOUT ANYTHING ELSE. HE HAS ONLY ONE LIFE, AND THAT'S BASEBALL. THAT WAY HE'S HAPPY, AND I'M HAPPY FOR HIM.[6]

—*Edna Stengel*

HE WAS BASEBALL'S GREATEST SALESMAN BECAUSE HE TREATED EVERYONE THE SAME.[7]

—*Sparky Anderson*

HE WAS WORTHLESS. WORTHLESS! A MANAGER WHO FALLS ASLEEP ON THE BENCH EVERY DAY—AND THIS IS NO EXAGGERATION—SHOULD NOT BE MANAGING IN THE BIG MAJORS. HE WAS THERE FOR NO OTHER REASON THAN TO ATTRACT FANS.[8]

—Ed Bouchee, Mets first baseman in 1963

HE'D TALK ALL NIGHT AND IF YOU WEREN'T A BASEBALL MAN YOU'D THINK THE GUY WAS CRAZY. BUT IF YOU WERE A BASEBALL MAN, WELL, BY THE TIME YOU FINALLY GOT TO BED—AND THE CHANCES ARE HE'D BE SITTING ON THE BED STILL TALKING—YOU DISCOVERED YOU WERE REALLY LEARNING THINGS. I MEAN YOU'D QUIT SECOND-GUESSING.[9]

—George Weiss, then Yankees general manager

HE'S A DRIVER ON SMALL DETAILS . . . JUST AS HE EXPECTS US TO WORK AT OUR JOBS, CASEY WORKED AT HIS. HE DIDN'T MISS MUCH. HIS PLATOON SYSTEM NOT ONLY KEPT US ON OUR TOES BUT GAVE US THE EQUIVALENT OF A DOZEN EXTRA MEN. THAT'S WHAT WINS PENNANTS.[10]

—Whitey Ford

Casey at the mike, spinning gold for the media.
(Courtesy of New York Yankees)

HE'S NOTHING BUT A CLOWN. HE WAS A CLOWN WHEN HE CAME AND HE'LL BE A CLOWN WHEN HE GOES.[11]

—*Joe Page, Yankees relief pitcher*
released by Stengel after 1950 season

I SWEAR, I DON'T UNDERSTAND SOME OF THE THINGS HE DOES WHEN HE MANAGES. I'VE TRIED TO FIGURE THEM OUT, BUT THEY JUST DON'T MAKE SENSE.[12]

—*Al Lopez, major league manager*

I WOULDN'T LET HIM IN MY HOUSE. I WOULDN'T WANT MY WIFE AND CHILDREN TO MEET HIM.[13]

—*unidentified disgruntled Mets player*

I WISH I HAD REALLY KNOWN CASEY STENGEL A LOT SOONER. IT WOULD HAVE MADE MY LIFE A LOT EASIER, A LOT HAPPIER. BUT I DIDN'T KNOW HIM, NOT REALLY, UNTIL MY LAST YEAR. I THOUGHT I DID. A LOT OF PLAYERS THOUGHT THEY DID. WE WERE WRONG.[14]

—*Jerry Coleman, former Yankees second baseman*

I PLAYED FOR CASEY BEFORE AND AFTER HE WAS A GENIUS.[15]

—*Warren Spahn, who played for Stengel when
he managed the Boston Braves and the New York Mets*

I NEVER HAD ANY TROUBLE WITH HIM. IF YOU PLAYED BALL HARD, KEPT YOUR MOUTH SHUT, AND HUSTLED, HE NEVER SAID MUCH TO YOU.[16]

—*Roger Maris*

HE WAS A FUNNY MAN. PUBLIC-RELATIONS WISE, HE WAS GOOD FOR BASEBALL. BUT HE DIDN'T GET ALONG WITH HIS VETERANS. HE WANTED A BUNCH OF YOUNG PLAYERS HE COULD CONTROL.[17]

—*Phil Rizzuto*

I LEARNED MORE BASEBALL AND HAD MORE FUN PLAYING ONE YEAR UNDER CASEY WITH THE METS THAN IN ANY OTHER SEASON IN MY CAREER.[18]

—*Richie Ashburn*

IF YOU DIDN'T LIKE CASEY, YOU DIDN'T LIKE ANYBODY.[19]

—*John Drebinger*, New York Times *sportswriter*

JOHN (MCGRAW) FOUND INTELLIGENT OFF-FIELD
COMPANIONSHIP IN DAVE BANCROFT AND CASEY. BOTH
HAD A GREAT SENSE OF HUMOR. I THINK JOHN
LAUGHED MORE WITH BANNY AND CASEY THAN WITH
ANYONE IN BASEBALL.[20]

—*Blanche McGraw, John McGraw's wife*

MY GOD, HE TALKS THE WAY JAMES JOYCE WRITES.[21]

—*unnamed sportswriter, after first meeting Casey*

SHAKE MY HAND? HE WASN'T EVEN THERE TO SAY
GOOD-BYE.[22]

—*Joe Page*

STENGELESE WAS MOSTLY A PUBLIC ACT. HE DOUBLE-TALKED
IN PART TO DIFFUSE PINPOINT QUESTIONS.[23]

—*Maury Allen, sportswriter*

THE MAN WHO DID THE MOST FOR BASEBALL IN BOSTON IN 1943 WAS THE MOTORIST WHO RAN STENGEL DOWN TWO DAYS BEFORE THE OPENING GAME AND KEPT HIM AWAY FROM THE BRAVES FOR TWO MONTHS.[24]

—Dave Egan, sportswriter

THE BIGGEST THING CASEY TAUGHT ME AS A MANAGER WAS TO PLAY BASEBALL ACCORDING TO YOUR PERSONNEL. IF YOU HAD POOR PITCHING AND HITTING, YOU HAD TO PLAY FOR BIG INNINGS. CASEY DIDN'T MANAGE FOR THE CROWD. HE MANAGED FOR THE PLAYERS AND MADE THE MOST OF THEIR ABILITIES.[25]

—Ralph Houk

THERE WAS NEVER A DAY AROUND CASEY WHEN I DIDN'T LAUGH.[26]

—Zach Wheat

WELL, SIRS AND LADIES, THE YANKEES HAVE NOW BEEN
MATHEMATICALLY ELIMINATED FROM THE 1949 PENNANT
RACE. THEY ELIMINATED THEMSELVES WHEN THEY ENGAGED
PERFESSER CASEY STENGEL TO MISMANAGE THEM FOR THE
NEXT TWO YEARS, AND YOU MAY BE SURE THAT THE PERFESS-
ER WILL OBLIGE TO THE BEST OF HIS UNIQUE ABILITY.[27]

—Dave Egan

WELL, GOD IS CERTAINLY GETTING AN EARFUL TONIGHT.[28]

*—Jim Murray, sportswriter, penning the
perfect eulogy upon Stengel's death in 1975*

YOU OPEN THE PAPER IN THE MORNING AND YOU READ
HOW LOUSY YOU ARE.[29]

*—Clete Boyer, on Casey's penchant for
discussing his players' weaknesses with the press*

YOUR ATTEMPT AT SUICIDE FULLY UNDERSTOOD. DEEPEST SYMPATHY YOU DIDN'T SUCCEED.[30]

> —*a telegram sent by Pirates manager Frankie Frisch to Braves manager Stengel after he was hit by a taxicab as he crossed the street in Boston during the 1943 season*

CASEY LIKED ME. I LIKED HIM. WE COULDN'T HAVE GOTTEN ALONG BETTER. HE WAS A LEFT-HANDER, TOO. WE UNDER-STOOD EACH OTHER.[31]

> —*Tommy Byrne, Yankees pitcher*

CASEY WAS THE BEST MANAGER I EVER PLAYED FOR. NO DOUBT ABOUT IT. ONE OF THE REASONS WAS (THAT) HE WAS SO HARD TO FIGURE OUT.[32]

> —*Billy Martin*

CASEY STENGEL—ONE OF THE DAFFIEST GUYS I EVER MET.[33]

> —*Babe Ruth*

NOTES

1 Opening Pitches

1. *New York World-Telegram*, June 14, 1935.
2. Berkow, Ira, and Jim Kaplan, *The Gospel According to Casey*. New York: St. Martin's Press, 1992.
3. *Saturday Evening Post*, September 30, 1961.
4. Halberstam, David, *Summer of '49*. New York: William Morrow, 1989.
5. Baseball World.
6. *Baseball Almanac*.
7. Freedomkeys.com.
8. Freedomkeys.com.
9. Creamer, Robert, *Stengel, His Life and Times*. Lincoln, NB: University of Nebraska Press, 1996.
10. *New York Post*, February 10, 1968.
11. Creamer.
12. Baseball World.
13. *The Sporting News*, October 18, 1975.
14. Berkow and Kaplan.
15. Bak, Richard, *Casey Stengel, A Splendid Baseball Life*. Dallas: Taylor Publishing, 1997.
16. Kahn, Roger, *The Era 1947–1957*. New York: Ticknor and Fields, 1993.
17. *Sports Illustrated*, October 13, 1975.
18. Creamer.
19. Freedomkeys.com.
20. Baseball World.
21. Ibid.
22. *Baseball Almanac*.
23. Ibid.
24. Baseball World.
25. Berkow and Kaplan.
26. Ibid.
27. *Baseball Almanac*.
28. Durso, Joe, *Casey, The Life and Legend of Charles Dillon Stengel*. Englewood Cliffs, NJ: Prentice Hall, 1967.

29. Baseball World.
30. *New York Post*, February 10, 1968.
31. Berkow and Kaplan.
32. Ibid.
33. Bak.
34. Berkow and Kaplan.
35. Bak.
36. Anderson, Dave, Murray Chass, Robert Creamer, and Harold Rosenthal, *The Yankees: The Four Fabulous Eras of Baseball's Most Famous Team*. New York, Random House, 1979.
37. Ibid.
38. Ibid.
39. Forker, Dom, *Men of Autumn: An Oral History of the 1949–53 World Champion New York Yankees*. Dallas: Taylor Publishing, 1989.
40. Ross, Alan, *The Yankees Century*. Nashville, TN: Cumberland House, 2001.

2 The Old Perfesser

1. *Baseball Almanac*.
2. Ibid.
3. Bak, Richard, *Casey Stengel, A Splendid Baseball Life*.
4. Berkow and Kaplan, *The Gospel According to Casey*.
5. *New York Times*, September 20, 1987.
6. *The Sporting News*, October 18, 1975.
7. *The Sporting News*, August 10, 1960.
8. Baseball World.
9. Bak.
10. Ibid.
11. *Baseball Almanac*.
12. Ibid.
13. Berkow and Kaplan.
14. Ibid.
15. Ibid.
16. Creamer, *Stengel, His Life and Times*.
17. Bak.
18. *Baseball Almanac*.
19. Berkow and Kaplan.
20. Ibid.
21. *Baseball Almanac*.

3 His Age and Health

1. Berkow and Kaplan, *The Gospel According to Casey.*
2. MacLean, Norman, *Casey Stengel.* New York: Drake Publishers, 1976.
3. Creamer, *Stengel, His Life and Times.*
4. *Baseball Almanac.*
5. Berkow and Kaplan.
6. *The Sporting News,* August 21, 1965.
7. Baseball World.
8. Berkow and Kaplan.
9. Baseball World.
10. Ibid.

4 His Playing Career

1. *Baseball Almanac.*
2. Berkow and Kaplan, *The Gospel According to Casey.*
3. Bak, Richard, *Casey Stengel, A Splendid Baseball Life.*
4. Ibid.
5. Berkow and Kaplan.
6. Bak.
7. Ibid.
8. *Saturday Evening Post,* July 31, 1965.
9. *Toledo Blade,* June 15, 1961.
10. Bak.
11. Freedomkeys.com.
12. *Baseball Almanac.*
13. *New York Times,* April 3, 1967.
14. Anderson et al, *The Yankees.*
15. MacLean, *Casey Stengel.*
16. Ibid.
17. Tullius, John, *I'd Rather Be a Yankee.* New York: MacMillan, 1986.
18. MacLean.

5 Managing

1. Allen, Maury, *Jackie Robinson, A Life Remembered.* Danbury, CT: Franklin Watts, 1987.
2. *New York Times,* February 27, 1954.
3. Durso, Casey, *The Life and Legend of Charles Dillon Stengel.*
4. *Baseball Almanac.*

Notes

5. Ibid.
6. Berkow and Kaplan, *The Gospel According to Casey*.
7. Creamer, *Stengel, His Life and Times*.
8. *Baseball Almanac*.
9. Ibid.
10. Ibid.
11. Ibid.
12. Ibid.
13. Berkow and Kaplan.
14. Creamer.
15. Berkow and Kaplan.
16. *Baseball Almanac*.
17. Creamer.
18. *Baseball Almanac*.
19. *Saturday Evening Post*, July 31, 1965.
20. Creamer.
21. Tullius, *I'd Rather Be a Yankee*.
22. Ibid.
23. Ross, *The Yankees Century*.
24. Forker, *The Men of Autumn*.

6 Players

1. Okrent, Daniel, and Steve Wulf, *Baseball Anecdotes*. New York: Harper Perennial, 1993.
2. *Baseball Almanac*.
3. Kahn, *The Era*.
4. Creamer, *Stengel, His Life and Times*.
5. Berkow and Kaplan, *The Gospel According to Casey*.
6. *New York Daily News*, February 3, 1959.
7. *Baseball Almanac*.
8. Okrent and Wulf.
9. Shecter, Leonard, "Bring Back the Real Mets!," reprinted in *The Armchair Book of Baseball*. Charles Scribner's Sons: New York, 1985.
10. Ibid.
11. Bak, *Casey Stengel, A Splendid Baseball Life*.
12. Berkow and Kaplan.
13. *Saturday Evening Post*, July 31, 1965.
14. Cramer, Ben, *Joe DiMaggio: The Hero's Life*. New York: Touchstone Books, 2001.

15. *New York Daily News*, April 19, 1987.
16. Creamer.
17. Berkow and Kaplan.
18. *The Sporting News*, August 10, 1960.
19. *Baseball Almanac.*
20. Berkow and Kaplan.
21. Bak.
22. *Baseball Almanac.*
23. Ibid.
24. Cramer.
25. Kahn.
26. Ibid.
27. *Baseball Almanac.*
28. Tullius, *I'd Rather Be a Yankee.*

7 The Yankees

1. Creamer, *Stengel, His Life and Times.*
2. *New York Journal-American*, November 11, 1952.
3. Berkow and Kaplan, *The Gospel According to Casey.*
4. Bak, *Casey Stengel, A Splendid Baseball Life.*
5. *Baseball Almanac.*
6. Kubek and Pluto, *Sixty-One.* New York: MacMillan, 1987.
7. Halberstam, *Summer of '49.*
8. *Baseball Almanac.*
9. Creamer.
10. *Baseball Almanac.*
11. Bak.
12. *The Sporting News*, February 18, 1959.
13. *New York Post*, March 1, 1956.
14. Creamer.
15. Ibid.
16. Bak.
17. Halberstam.
18. Berkow and Kaplan.
19. Associated Press, September 1, 1966.
20. Berkow and Kaplan.
21. Creamer.
22. *Baseball Almanac.*
23. Cramer.

24. *Baseball Almanac.*
25. Berkow and Kaplan.
26. Creamer.
27. *New York Journal-American*, August 21, 1965.
28. Creamer.
29. *New York Daily News*, April 19, 1987.
30. *Baseball Almanac.*
31. Kubek and Pluto.
32. Anderson et al, *The Yankees.*
33. MacLean, *Stengel.*
34. Forker, *The Men of Autumn.*
35. Tullius, *I'd Rather Be a Yankee.*
36. Ibid., excerpted from *Casey at the Bat*, by Casey Stengel, New York: Random House, 1961.
37. Tullius.
38. Ibid.
39. Ross, Alan, *The Yankees Century.*
40. Ibid.
41. Ibid.

8 The Amazin' Mets

1. Berkow and Kaplan, *The Gospel According to Casey.*
2. Creamer, *Stengel, His Life and Times.*
3. *Baseball Almanac.*
4. Berkow and Kaplan.
5. Creamer.
6. Ibid.
7. Ibid.
8. Ibid.
9. Ibid.
10. Berkow and Kaplan.
11. Creamer.
12. Ibid.
13. *Sports Illustrated*, October 6, 1962.
14. Shecter, "Bring Back the Real Mets!"
15. Berkow and Kaplan.
16. *Sports Illustrated*, August 13, 1962.
17. Creamer.
18. Berkow and Kaplan.

19. Creamer.
20. Ibid.
21. *New York Times*, February 24, 1962.
22. Creamer.
23. *New York Post*, March 25, 1964.
24. Baseball World.
25. *The Sporting News*, March 7, 1962.
26. *New York Journal-American*, August 24, 1963.
27. *Baseball Almanac*.
28. Bak, *Casey Stengel, A Splendid Baseball Life*.
29. *New York Journal-American*, August 24, 1963.
30. *Baseball Almanac*.
31. *Sports Illustrated*, August 13, 1962.
32. *The Sporting News*, June 9, 1962.
33. *New York Times*, June 19, 1969.
34. Shecter.
35. *Baseball Almanac*.
36. Shecter.
37. Ibid.
38. Baseball World.
39. Creamer.
40. Berkow and Kaplan.
41. Ibid.
42. *The Sporting News*, March 7, 1962.
43. *New York Times*, July 13, 1986.
44. MacLean, *Casey Stengel*.

9 Others on Casey

1. *Saturday Evening Post*, July 31, 1965.
2. *The Sporting News*, October 18, 1975.
3. Creamer, *Stengel, His Life and Times*.
4. *Washington Post*, May 8, 1949.
5. Bak, *Casey Stengel, A Splendid Baseball Life*.
6. Creamer.
7. Berkow and Kaplan, *The Gospel According to Casey*.
8. Bak.
9. Creamer.
10. *Toledo Blade*, June 18, 1961.
11. Creamer.

Notes

12. Ibid.
13. *New York Journal-American*, May 23, 1963.
14. *New York Daily News*, July 23, 1965.
15. Berkow and Kaplan.
16. Bak.
17. Forker, *The Men of Autumn*.
18. Bak.
19. Creamer.
20. *New York Daily News*, October 19, 1960.
21. *Sports Illustrated*, October 13, 1975.
22. *Saturday Evening Post*, July 31, 1965.
23. Bak.
24. *Boston Record*, October 12, 1943.
25. Berkow and Kaplan.
26. Creamer.
27. *Boston Record*, October 13, 1948.
28. *Los Angeles Times*, September 30, 1975.
29. *Saturday Evening Post*, July 31, 1965.
30. Bak.
31. Forker.
32. Ibid.
33. Tullius, *I'd Rather Be a Yankee*.